FOOLS & TRAMPS

by Karen Kellock Ph.D.

Manual for Superior Men

A complete theory based on Einstein physics,
Political Psychology, Systems Theory
and Archetypal Psychiatry.

FORMULA

All success attraction
All disease obstruction
All recovery elimination

You must fast on all three

OBSTRUCTIONS:

People
Habit
Food

FOOLS & TRAMPS

Most importantly beloved, stay away from people. Be the top 5% and have nothing to do with evil. We must now divide from their ranks. Reject, give God thanks.   Living in a small liberal town was like being part of a huge dysfunctional family: treachery.   If you don't fit their thing they will blame you for everything but insiders get off free see. They can't help doing wrong. Tho' they flourish like the olive tree tomorrow they're all mowed down.

FOOLS FORSAKEN

NARCISSISM: SPIRIT OF THE DEVIL
IT'S A TRAUMA BOND
GIVE UP FUTURE VISIONS OF HIM
DEVALUATION HURTS
HE KEEPS YOU ON CONSTANT ALERT
PROTEIN DEPRIVATION

FOOLS FORSAKEN

Take his lovebombs about how great you are and immortalize them as truth, the rest IGNORE.

A queen never chases/begs a man! If he's unavailable that's it--she never thinks of him again.

Those who go along to get along : that's the worst betrayal of humanity. Holocaust survivor.

Narcissists identified by how they make you feel. Anxious, fearful, self-questioning? then it's real.

Young women [vacuous but pretty] have high SMV. Just that shows you the state of men today.

NARCISSISM: SPIRIT OF THE DEVIL

The spirit of narcissism is the devil. He's arrogant, deceptive and selfish like all demons below.

His grandiosity makes the alert sick. He's transparent yet making it--but that's not the end of it.

He becomes a completely different person at will, but that's also a pattern making you sick still.

The cure is to be on about your life. Individuate, MATURE, don't ever fall for these types.

He will never love you cuz that's not how he's made up Sue. Get that central, no future fakes too.

Don't waste time/decades groveling before rejecting men: trauma bonded as cycles repeat again.

CUT IT OFF NOW. From these words you see it all so there's no reason to continue in this fail.

FOOLS FORSAKEN

IT'S A TRAUMA BOND

It's a TRAUMA BOND and that's why he's in every groveling thought. Looking "up to" the slob.

He ignores you, doesn't talk to you but talks to others: cut it off now before a trauma bond flowers.

You run every thought by him as if he's in the room--but he will NEVER be: it's a trauma bond see.

The more unavailable he is the more addictive to a girl stuck in early trauma and thus defective.

He lies about everything and you know it. His grandiosity makes you sick but you stuff it.

GIVE UP FUTURE VISIONS OF HIM

Give up future fakes about him being with you. He will NEVER be with you, he's a mirage of lies Sue.

The silent treatment is a narcissist's main punishment. So be it, walk away before you're addicted.

He may be silent with you for MONTHS. Enjoy the silence or communicate with someone else.

He's silent but never tells you what you did wrong. Time to pack your stuff up and move along.

One narc's silent treatment is another narc's rage. Either way you're up a creek with him ok.

He may start speeding cuz you did something--anything to scare you. Call support and get out Sue.

His other punishment is the Smear Campaign. He seeks to wreck your rep and ruin you ok.

FOOLS FORSAKEN

The smear campaign starts during the relationship but accelerates after. They just do this, traitors.

The preemptively smear campaign when they have someone else/need excuse to reject ok.

DEVALUATION HURTS

They start to value you less and you feel it. Withholding affection, that touch--all of that is absent.

Emotional intimacy is withdrawn as punishment and that's just another one: don't cry, move on.

Never fret when the narcissist shines for he'll pull himself down--that's a pattern too, aye.

He slobbers for attention, he craves admiration--so he'll go worldly to get it, to his destruction.

They sought to bring me down and I let em--by getting drunk at them. This was my youth, amen.

If you don't speak up you're complicit with evil. If they go along with the crowd drop those people.

Anger, hatred and envy is the dark triad of narcissists. They're always there despite acting nice.

When someone likes to see you cry and suffer you know it's a narcissist and none other.

He triggers this, it's part of the syndrome. Triggering bad feelings about yourself or your role.

A continuous state of alert or fear. This is what they do: trigger you until sickness/death are near.

God put you in dire social situations to overcome them and give you an edge: it was necessary son.

FOOLS FORSAKEN

Social muscle: it's what you lacked in the past. You trusted too easily and caved in when bashed.

If on protein only you can eat thrice a week. Three meals with full & happy satiation in between.

HE KEEPS YOU ON CONSTANT ALERT

Alert: the narcissist keeps you on constant alert cuz even when he loves you he's gonna turn.

An older woman has higher value to God & family but men arrogantly say "yes but she has low SMV".

SMV--Sexual Market Value--has nothing to do with true value so it's dangerous for men too.

Find--be attracted to--a man who sees your true value not your sexual market value which is cruel.

Did the Queen of England have low SMV? A billionaire, a leader of nations for > half a century?

It is the older women who educate the younger women in morality, something untaught today.

PROTEIN DEPRIVATION

No energy, no immunity, skin goes to hell and whole body swells: kwashiorkor--protein is nil.

Dander alert. If you're a pet lover you're not gonna eliminate em so we adapt to friends with fur.

FOOLS DESCRIBED

NARCISSISTS ARE A CONSTANT FIGHT
YOU'RE DESIGNED FOR A PURPOSE
BLOCK THOUGHTS ON THE BUM
TRICKS ON THE MIND
HOLD YOUR HEAD/BOUNDARIES HIGH
BOUNDARY BUSTING INCREASES
WHY NO CONTACT
DIVERSITY IS A LICENTIOUS MADHOUSE
COVER NARCISSISTS CAN'T HEAR YOU
THEY WANT WHATEVER YOU HAVE
EVIL IS ALWAYS MASKED

FOOLS DESCRIBED

It's a healthy shock to learn that your friends don't want you to succeed, but see it.

My knowledge comes adversity more than anything else in school: it built character see.

NARCISSISTS ARE A CONSTANT FIGHT

It was a constant fight with a narcissist in the house. Even my own viewpoints were disallowed.

It's very Christian to see the wild nature of people. They're so bad it's inconceivable.

Put your armor on every morning. See the human condition for what it is then start winning.

Great queens held down by bums and she's so obsessed he's disgusted as she falls down.

See the perp as heroin. You gotta stay away for your very life, withdraw, begin again.

You always saw him as a pathetic phony but somehow he got you under his spell anyway.

YOU'RE DESIGNED FOR A PURPOSE

You're designed for a purpose/to do something great but are blocked, so go no contact.

Every time you switch thoughts from the perp to you [the First] it's sudden growth, a lot.

Lovebombing is designed to lock you in and make you so afraid of losing it you'll do anything.

FOOLS DESCRIBED

When times were bad, reflecting on love at the beginning kept you stuck in this den gone black.

Just like heroin the withdrawal is painful but then with each day you get more powerful.

You were degraded and didn't know it. You were under his spell and really showed it.

Go thru withdrawal or you're not number one. You're dependent on one who sees you as a peon.

BLOCK THOUGHTS ON THE BUM

You're inferior to no one but the way they carried on made you feel low/in a dark dungeon.

You've gotta think so much of yourself you drop the bum and no going back to check on hell.

You already knew he's not interested in you so thought less of yourself but NOT if you're through.

You can either have "him" or your destiny and the latter brings pleasure so choose rightly.

Block thoughts on him and switch to your great future and splendid work for the heathen.

If that bum gets your attention again chastise yourself and go back to that great queen within.

TRICKS ON THE MIND

The devil plays tricks with your mind so if you go back you'll see a great prince who's kind.

If you lurk he'll be looking so great with new supply at the gate so stay home and you won't deflate.

FOOLS DESCRIBED

Realize that no-contact means no-see/hear too for images and sounds are powerful for you.

Be stronger than your addiction As self respect returns it gets much easier I reckon.

For every minute you don't go back it's filling up with things pertaining to you, queen at top.

When obsessed it includes how they dress, what they say or eat and all their dam relatives.

Imagine all this mental energy released back to you and your great and marvelous destiny!

You get so good at switching back to you it gets fun and you understand how its done.

HOLD YOUR HEAD/BOUNDARIES HIGH

A Christian sees a fallen world, that most are evil: a flood going to hell but to heaven just a trickle.

It truly is a school of hard knocks, what I call Ph.D. in the Streets: how to navigate the peeps.

Make your boundaries so high that people know you won't tolerate anything coming against you.

Narcissists bust boundaries as they feel entitled to do what they want and don't care about effects.

They push you to put up with things until your boundaries no longer exist: that's the gist.

If he is too immature to navigate relationships he'll give you the silent treatment which increases.

The silent treatments are more frequent and last longer: see patterns or continue to suffer.

FOOLS DESCRIBED

He busts your boundaries by monopolizing all of your time and getting mad if you draw the line.

They get mad if you want time to yourself. They see it as selfishness as far as I can tell.

I felt I never had time to myself anymore as he would come and go: my life was disordered.

BOUNDARY BUSTING INCREASES

Allow him to break that boundary just once and soon he's doing it all the time you dunce.

Sleepless nights of frustration and rage alternate with making this sick relationship ok.

Narcissists rage when you see things differently because you're an extension of them they think.

Over time you agree with them just to keep the peace but then the rage builds inside see.

The world violates your boundaries if you're unclear on them or your unique wants and needs.

Even after careful explanation of your limits their behavior won't change [socially deranged].

They push the limits on what is acceptable until they get their way: it's totally exhausting ok.

The past was just actors put there for your education. They're dead or gone now so stop reliving it.

It's like training a child only you can't train him. He never learns cuz he wants his way, amen?

Gaslighting. They always question your sanity and make you doubt your decisional ability.

FOOLS DESCRIBED

Getting you to doubt your own judgement hands control over to him, the narc belligerent.

You're shocked and bring up red flags but he says you're imagining things/denies it flat.

WHY NO CONTACT

If they loved you you'd be happy and you wouldn't have to go no contact, so remember that.

Don't degrade yourself by ever looking back and every time you think of him remember that.

With each day your True Self illuminates stronger as you de-attach from a real bummer.

You weren't loved like you wanted so break the spell by going no contact [way outa hell].

The love spell is tunnel-vision so as you open up you see a whole new horizon--amazin'!

Suddenly you regain sights/smells from childhood, released from his spell with it all understood.

Going no-contact puts you back on top, not always chasing him and sucking/looking up.

Looking up to someone who doesn't care about you is so demeaning and destiny-destroying too.

Women should stay close to loved ones not venture out and chase some silly apathetic man.

Stay home woman, make environment reflect your personality and never think of him again.

Get it thru your head he doesn't care and love yourself enough to get the hell outa there.

FOOLS DESCRIBED

For love is not a game and you could get seriously hurt with a destructive soul tie ok.

Soul ties are sexual: it's nature's way of reproducing by keeping the attraction consensual.

But the sex instinct is also expanded to proliferate a sick race--the love addict is sick ok?

If you dis-attend from the bum the thoughts will eventually stop cuz God doesn't want you down.

If you lurk on his page, self-forgive and start again: you know this keeps you down my friend.

You always knew he was a phony with fake intelligence but somehow got hooked nevertheless.

God saw the whole thing and knew what was happening but it was a lesson for your destiny.

Now get into YOUR thing/music/past times and never "look up to" the apathetic again, aye.

It's cookie cutter intelligence vs. your True Self inside, what is called inborn Aesthetic Knowledge.

DIVERSITY IS A LICENTIOUS MADHOUSE

Diversity is a licentious madhouse so get ready for confusion, depression and insults.

People hang with their own but if whites do that it's evil supremacy: has logic totally gone?

I wasn't good enough. A scared, bullied, abused child who later got whole and tough.

FOOLS DESCRIBED

Your gift is so unique and highly specialized you gotta be alone to expand/not be compromised.

Push your limits cuz there's always more. Soon a 100 mile race seems like 50 and it's not a chore.

Sin will cost you more/keep you longer than you planned. Sometimes decades are lost man.

Most sins are devices to avoid anxiety. But then they cause more until you're in a dark infinity.

You don't build a nation by hiding the truth for that only destroys it sooner or later too.

COVER NARCISSISTS CAN'T HEAR YOU

The minute you start talking about yourself not them they drift off--you feel you're never enough.

They can't help themselves. When you talk they will either yawn or roll their eyes a lot.

If he didn't choose you as number one with no other groupies around then dump him now.

Going no contact with a psychopath opens you up to a whole new world with you on top.

Incredibly rude, frustrating but also frightening because envy can send us in a tailspin.

They expect to be heard but when it's your turn to talk they can't keep up or go dense/weird.

They hate you as a lazy bum, they hate you when you're workin and hate you when succeeding.

For success stay free of the unpleasant past and present pests. Now clear you can re-adjust.

FOOLS DESCRIBED

Less intelligent people are prone to overestimate their competence while genius feels less.

One cannot fake genuine intelligence and when he tries everyone can see he's a dunce.

It's the Law of Reciprocity: if they give you a gift you're obligated so it may not be good see.

Stop remorsing over "shoulda dones". You did it so repeated recall is destructive hon'.

He says you're way too sensitive and laughs it off. That is the way it is with that lot.

THEY WANT WHATEVER YOU HAVE

Whatever you have they want. If you have two it's give me one, losing things on the playground.

You're not allowed to have more, that's what makes communism so miserable/always dictators.

Statistics show white men as most tolerant and all women as free speech bashing tyrants.

What you say is a reason to hate you. If they don't understand it it's "harming" them too.

Conservatives welcome healthy debate, liberals do not--they wanna shut you up now ok.

As part of the debate club I loved hearing all views. Bring em out/flush em out, evolve to new.

Conservatives welcome healthy debate, liberals do not--they wanna shut you up/call you nuts.

You're "harming" them if they're jealous of your hard work--can this crap get any worse?

FOOLS DESCRIBED

They don't work as hard as you so you gotta hide your assiduity so they won't feel blue.

There's nothing higher than your own mind so turn off the outer, open to the divine and write.

There's nothing to fear unless you're in sin for our loving Father in heaven disciplines.

EVIL IS ALWAYS MASKED

Evil human nature is always masked behind a purified image and that's like cultural neurosis.

The competition anxiety in women is beyond the pale. It's. destructive and we're going down ok.

My story was like Blanche in Streetcar: I was supersensitive mal-adapting to grosser relatives.

Jezebel gets her men to do the dirty work on her enemies and it can get atrocious/nasty.

Since the narcissist has no empathy when you confront with feelings he will reject your reality.

He has confirmation bias--confirming only his views--so of course he'll reject feelings from you.

FOOLS & TRAMPS

PSYCHOTIC WITH TRAUMA
GASLIGHTING
CONTRIVED CONFUSION
MEMORIES ARE ANCHORS
AS HER VALUE PLUMMETS
LOVEBOMBED BY IDIOTS
DRIVEN BY A CLEVER CLOWN
FEMALE INSANITY IS CREATED
BREADCRUMBING
WISHING AND HOPING FOREVER
CHOOSE YOUR PAIN
THE GROUP IS UNSELF-AWARE
LUNATIC MOBS
THE IMMATURE ARE DENSE FOR SURE
SOUL TIES AND TOXIC HOPE
PLAYING YOUR MIND, EMOTIONS, WILL
BJ ARTIST IN TOWN
ONE SIDED RELATIONSHIPS
ARE YOU SITTING IN PIG PIES
ANXIETY IS AN ACHING GUT
BE YOUR CHILD AGAIN
YOU MAL-ADAPTED TO DYSFUNCTION
IDENTITY IS RELATIONAL
WITHOUT RIGID MORALS
FIRST THEY LOOK GOOD
YOU'RE CALLED A "CONTROLLER"
MICROCHEATING
MICRO-CHEATING ISN'T SEX

FOOLS & TRAMPS

MALIGNANT FEMALE NARCISSIST
PASSIVE AGGRESSIVE ACTIONS
GUT ACHES FROM UNSTABLE GUYS
STOP THINKING PAST LOWLIFES
AMORAL YOUTH SO UNCOUTH
DEFEATED BRATS SITTING IN WHITE
REESTABLISH THE OLD PATHS
NO DOCTRINE JUST VIRTUE SIGNALING
THE NEW CRAPPY WORLD
THE NEW CRAPPY WOMEN
RUNAWAY FEMALES IN POWER
FEMALE TYRANNY IS SO COMMON TODAY
IT'S CRUEL WHEN EMOTION RULES
BLESSED MONOTONY IS FUN FOR ME
WOMEN, BE REASONABLE FOR A CHANGE
FORGET THE PAST, LOOK FORWARD TO A BLAST
SEEK STABLE MEN
SUDDEN SUCCESS!
DUNNING-KRUGER AND AOC CORTEZ
YOUTH LACK CRITICAL THINKING
YOUNG SOCIALISTS PISSED
GOD WILL TAKE CARE OF IT—DON'T WORRY!
FORGIVE TO BE FREE OF THEM!
FOR SPIRITUAL SOLACE—CHURCHES?
AOC IS RACIST TO WHITE MEN
SEASONS OF LIFE
LOVING PEOPLE MEANS MERCY
UNRESOLVED ANGER: BLOW UPS
IS THIS ONE?

FOOLS & TRAMPS

FOOLS & TRAMPS

PSYCHOTIC WITH TRAUMA

She's psychotic with trauma from all here discussed: just an empty vessel they wanted to lock up.

You went thru a very dark place but the war is over see. Put it in the lowest ocean & don't go fishing.

God rescued you from that dark world so why keep resenting it? There are TWO realities not one.

Any saint with a gift of tears elects to stay home because every dam thing triggers it dear.

Ubiquitous, condescending and completely untrue. That's the liberal mindset plaguing you.

It's such a temptation to go back and bitch again cuz we're in a better situation but don't son.

Her mind works overtime and she reads between the lines. They call her paranoid all the time.

Here you're designed by God to be a queen taking dominion but you're just a bum's minion.

The gaslighting syndrome of confusion and hate is designed to put one in a puppet like state.

GASLIGHTING

Gaslighting: He twists the whole argument around and now she's the one to blame/apologizing.

FOOLS & TRAMPS

Gaslighting purpose: If I can confuse you I can continue to use you. Get what I want/no intimacy too.

He's not the problem honey YOU are, so he will marry you when you finally get yourself together.

It's the Spirit of Confusion dragging you into it's vortex: you're caught up in an addictive love hex.

When a woman gets swept up in a sexual soul tie she really believes it's permanent/forever, aye.

And here the dude never had any intention of going beyond the lovebomb-discard symptom.

Keeping her in confusion, avoiding intimacy at all costs, no intention of marrying just bombing love.

For God is not the author of the confusion you're caught up in. It's a user's weapon but you're done.

CONTRIVED CONFUSION

This contrived confusion fogs the mind and blocks God's signals. He gives a way out but to no avail.

Being smitten with this situation tracks the mind into endless repetition and it's insane lookin'.

Love is the most addictive of all. It consumes every minute until our personal flame is small.

Whenever there's confusion in a situation you know God's not in it and so you reject it son.

Wherever there is envying and strife there is confusion in every work--get alert to this spirit/curse.

In confusion you begin to doubt your own judgement so as to rely on theirs and that is The End.

FOOLS & TRAMPS

Stop reviewing weak past thru present eyes of strength cuz it only brings frustration/resentment.

That was your Ph.D in the Streets, it was bad, now let it go: you had to endure ALL of it to know.

With every recall of how you gave in to that cave man you worshipped then you drown in adrenalin.

MEMORIES ARE ANCHORS

Everyone has memories they wish they didn't have: universalize this feeling of self-disgust love.

Don't drill down to past events only to drown in body chemicals with no immunity to rascals.

Never show your desperation for it always ends badly or you attract wrongly [I learned this early].

The smart man conserves energy to be ready for all emergencies: past anger is a waste see.

Confusion is the biggest energy waster. Every waking minute tracking this environment of fear.

Confusion IS the gaslighting. "Keep em on their toes to keep em confused" is a motto of schoolboys.

You tell me my thinking is wrong so now I deny my own judgement and rely on you for solutions.

All the while they've isolated you making you paranoid too and accepting that the problem is YOU.

You fall into a pit based on doubting your own judgement. It is grey, dark and nondescript.

Svengali's friends don't think she's so hot, a confused idiot who is needy, weak and cries a lot.

FOOLS & TRAMPS

AS HER VALUE PLUMMETS

As her value plummets he treats her worse and she's cursed--pray for clarity/God's reverse.

I've been there. I lost all my identity, values bashed, history forgotten, name ruined and trashed.

All over a clown who didn't have a right to a conversation even. All because I let him in.

A sliding interactional scale: we make gods out of people to the degree we lose our own value.

A gnawing inner homesickness for something, quieted with food, drugs, alcohol or that guy see.

All I knew was I was only happy alone in my room, free of the constant pressure to conform too.

I didn't like it when they came, I just felt pressured to do, think and endure their thing: boring!

I see now how doubting my own judgement put me in the darkest lowest place possible, amen.

LOVEBOMBED BY IDIOTS

All due to some soul tie to an idiot who managed to trick you into being complicit with the illicit.

Learn this and you'll agree there is nothing more important than boundaries: NOTHING.

For you are you and they are them but you got it confused with porous boundary/lines dim.

I'll never forget conforming to what I didn't want to, the feeling inside going against all I knew.

FOOLS & TRAMPS

I couldn't trust my own judgement so what else did I have, I had to trust someone didn't I love?

Years in a mental cocoon you'll never get back: don't see them as a waste, just tell all about it.

It's the dogged persistence of such relationships that define them. So it took years, forget it ma'am.

It's the dogged persistence of alcoholism and food addictions that define them: just go on.

DRIVEN BY A CLEVER CLOWN

A clown shrewdly implanted himself where he can now manage your entire life, a journey of fright.

Loveboming, avoiding intimacy and gaslighting are mind control: How to control to reach your goal.

It was taught in barber shops how to control women and it was sport to see how many succumbed.

She's crazy for even thinking this way. She's seeing things wrong and needs my direction ok.

The driver to this maneuver is to breakup or act like her trippin' is impossible to live with nonstop.

He says "it's over" and she bites the bullet to hold it together then he throws crumbs to the beggar.

Breadcrumbing is giving just enough to make her think there's a chance while remaining distant.

Breadcrumbing: he keeps a tie while remaining emotionally unavailable and it's hell ya know.

Breadcrumbing is similar to ghosting save the crumbs. He drops you then sends an email of love.

FOOLS & TRAMPS

FEMALE INSANITY IS CREATED

Love Bombing then avoiding intimacy and gaslighting is the driver of female insanity, undoubtedly.

The guy knows where her heart is so keeps dropping those crumbs as long as she's asleep.

Until she wakes up and gets off this degrading ride she's still saying "it's gonna happen this time".

She keeps falling for it as friends say "she's crazy" and the vortex sucks her down to hell see.

Quit dwelling on the lessons getting you here. They were way too painful and humiliating dear.

The impact of breadcrumbing [give a little then pull back] is what we call the Approval Trap.

Many approve of her but she wants he who rejects and continues to reject her with this behavior.

She spends the rest of her life seeking the approval of the man who broke her: how weird.

She wants the man who broke her to come back and fix her--the Approval Trap is a real bummer.

Don't waste your time. The person who breaks you is not he who's gonna come back and heal you.

BREADCRUMBING

From lovebombing to not relating, gaslighting and breadcrumbing: disengage now, quickly.

Tho' these are svengali tactics they're taught to men by past generations on how to control women.

FOOLS & TRAMPS

"Throw her a bone". How derogatory like she's a needy dog but you can see the life of a female alone.

Now we see how pimps can talk her into selling her body and giving him all the money, it's this surely.

And this is how a Ph.D. woman is manipulated by a bum: he knows these tactics passed on.

How has this process made her into a dope? Simply put, it has adhered her to a false hope.

He comes back again, "God has touched me" but hope deferred makes a heart even sicker friend.

WISHING AND HOPING FOREVER

Wishing and hoping for something that never comes makes us sick on the inside in the long run.

Where your treasure is your heart follows. You've invested so much it confirms false hopes.

Your heart is where your treasure is: you've invested so much it's almost impossible to leave it.

I have been hoodwinked but now I must cut my losses and move forward with my life, and fast.

He starts the cycle all over again but now you're a wizened woman and you break this pattern.

Look at it this way: your soul is sick and that person has handlebars driving you everywhere ok.

There's only ONE way to end this sick cycle. Separate yourself immediately from this one, NOW.

As long as your salivating and waiting for crumbs you are being ruled and tortured by a bum.

FOOLS & TRAMPS

No long counseling session. You're not giving this person access to your time and energy again.

You accept it for what it is, realize it's gonna hurt, choose your pain and know what comes first.

Choose between a wasted life and temporary pain of separating from an undeserving bum, aye.

CHOOSE YOUR PAIN

There's pain either way. Separating from a wrong person in heartbreak or going on with a fake.

Don't let your life pass by on a merry go round. Going fast, going nowhere and keeping you down.

It all comes down to one way out and an insight from God [His kiss]: I deserve better than this!

Until she decides to grow beyond dysfunction and leave the bum there's nothing else to say in sum.

THE GROUP IS UNSELF-AWARE

They're unself-aware, that's why they go to war on your novel views when they don't have a clue.

The leader and her monkeys still hate you but it has no effect now, we see the patterns all along.

Removing consequences (that's the big one) people learn to make impulsive, immature, poor decisions.

We no longer let their abuse, gaslighting, hurtful words cutting or gossiping to make us unhappy.

Always remember we are better people due to this toxic experience: growing, transforming successes.

FOOLS & TRAMPS

It's a choice: Choosing to be a better person is our choice not sinking in our swill, angry/pissed.

From that bad experience we built conscious awareness of ourselves: how we look, act and come off.

We are more careful than other people, acutely aware of how fast things can change/human evil.

Going thru a social war taught us acute attention to detail so that we never lose again to upheaval.

LUNATIC MOBS

The super rich must hang out together not from snobbery but due to the Dunning Kruger.

Procrustean conformity: amputating a leg to fit an iron bed, i.e. destroying ourselves to fit instead.

Dunning-Kruger: the dire effects of the smart adapting to the dumb when you literally must lie to them.

How do you conquer a people? By making them all EQUAL then they're finally controllable.

In free capitalism people are allowed and encouraged to stand out but no more, that's abhorred.

All I have to know is that I LIKE something, that's all. The subconscious selects, it KNOWS.

THE IMMATURE ARE DENSE FOR SURE

Before this happened I was so naive about human nature it's amazing I survived so immature.

People are cruel and they'll kill you thru the group to look innocent with their flying monkeys too.

FOOLS & TRAMPS

Shame is the most uncomfortable emotion humans can experience yet your own sisters imputed it.

With recovery we study the dynamics of abuse no longer being stuck in these systems too.

When treated poorly--malicious and vicious--it doesn't say who we are but volumes on them sis.

When they would yelled at me I naturally felt inferior in some way, never that they may be crazy.

They seemed to hate me--I must be heinous, egregious. They tell others to hate me--I deserve it see.

That kind of a social warlike situation has created a new creature in you: futuristic, a genius too.

Their unreasonable hate and hostility speaks volumes about who they are way down their evil core.

You have chosen joy, kindness and peace and that makes you far superior don't you think?

The healed victim is a perfect person and a magnet to other empaths and kindhearted sensitives.

SOUL TIES AND TOXIC HOPE

People struggle rejecting relationships that do everything but kill them: the bottomless cavern

This lethal struggle to move on and beyond is common and gets more abusive as the years go on.

You envisioned him as your future--new life with a wide scope--but he turned out to be "toxic hope".

It hurts to give up a dream/be left with nothing--the same sad lonely scene--so we stay with him.

FOOLS & TRAMPS

Rather than be left with nothing we persevere with him and deny what we see/feel/hear: sins.

Tho' all your investments were never reciprocated there is still that soul tie: aex demon of the night.

The glue of relationship is greater than attraction: a person nearly kills you and you stay with him?

He does everything but spit in her face and she's begging and holding on to him, it's disgustin'

There's something deeper than mere emotional for her to act like that, it's eerily psycho-spiritual.

The soul is mind, will and emotions. Soul tie: these come under the auspices of a svengali.

PLAYING YOUR MIND, EMOTIONS, WILL

He plays with her **MIND**, dictates her **EMOTIONS** and steers her **WILL**. A soul tie is from hell.

This person is not God's best, not even in His will, not God ordained and not anointed, so hell!

Stop trying to make it work/walk out once and for all. How to release a soul tie is what it's about.

Sibling abuse is a real thing and it happens in the deep dark recesses of family privacy: secrecy.

Who else haters gonna hate, someone they don't know? No, it's someone close, taking a terrible toll.

Finally, the estate attorney colluded with the enemy: the insider sisters and their flying monkeys.

The gruesome twosome elder sisters colluded with anyone who'd assist them or just listen.

FOOLS & TRAMPS

They colluded with attorneys, therapists, neighbors and family all to put me in my place forever see.

But I got the last word by writing these books about the turds: social psychology. I turned it to good.

It's not the queens disease it's the disempowered, sin-filled, victimized, voiceless girl's escape.

The queen couldn't drink, she'd be locked up. She couldn't use, she'd get ug. What's left, food.

Self-forgiveness results in next discovery: how they treated you honey but you were in denial see.

I've forgiven myself Jane, I've gone on ahead. I sense you don't want that, you want me dead.

BJ ARTIST IN TOWN

Women want approval, men want that. It's as obvious as can be but silly woman can't see it.

She's the greatest BJ artist in town and all the men are knocking her door down: it's a crime hon.

It's not fair to their sweet, godly wives. They're queens who won't be degraded save God fated it.

The thing to remember: the new life will be wonderful compared to the old one, quite miserable.

There was a desire in his heart that pulled him away from what was right and wholesome ok.

Somehow this soul tie relationship steered her away from anything wholesome--it was tragic.

That's the nasty soul tie: we lose our good judgment to pursue desires then put up with the liars.

FOOLS & TRAMPS

Lose good judgment and then tie yourself to the people of the land. What a terrible nightmare man.

The prodigal son left father and home to pursue desires in his heart by tying himself thru sex alone.

Thru sex he enjoined himself to the people of that town and lost his father's guidance and wisdom.

ONE SIDED RELATIONSHIPS

These new relationships wasted everything he had before leaving the boy humiliated and sad.

These new relationships were not reciprocal: he wasted his substance in riotous living that's all.

Here's the gist: His only way out of that situation was to leave it fast. Relocate, move now, go back.

He had to forget all his mistakes and the money he'd invested in an ugly emotional wasteland.

He had to forget everything of the recent and just leave it. No soul ties, simply walk away stupid.

Before he could leave and survive it he had to wake-up to it. You must wake up before you walk out.

The bible makes it clear he did not change until he woke up to himself--by looking at his outcomes.

ARE YOU SITTING IN PIG PIES

He was sitting in pig pies starving while his father's servants ate deliciously: he woke up mentally.

All the boy needed to do to wake up was to look around at his results. You gotta wake up to walk out.

FOOLS & TRAMPS

In the same way you thought you had a king but see he's a clown. He wears a raggedy hat not a crown.

You plant but harvest little, you eat not having enough, you clothe yourself but sleep cold/rough.

Your bags have holes in em cuz God says: he withheld his blessing until you considered your ways.

Think about what you're doing, how you're investing in slop--what have you gotten back? Naught.

Living in a small liberal town was like being part of a huge dysfunctional family: treachery.

Because they are so utterly self-involved they are ignorant, vacuous--they only have flash.

If you don't fit their thing they will blame you for everything but insiders get off Scot free.

Assert your right as an elder to state the truth to the uncouth youth. Hold back and the future goes black.

ANXIETY IS AN ACHING GUT

Anxiety is an aching gut as the solar plexus detects danger around us which is pandemic sis.

They can't help doing wrong. Tho' they flourish like the olive tree tomorrow they're all mowed down.

Stop talking about people. People-worshipping is boring with constant name dropping, evil!

For it's an INNER JOURNEY of adventure and enlightenment not socially adapting man.

Now you march to another beat you seem strange to them and that's another obstruction.

FOOLS & TRAMPS

I'm done with the outer life so don't invite me to your party tonight. I'm an introvert alright?

To all boring name droppers: You're supposed to love GOD first not people who are downers.

They always gotta be talking and they can't stand silence. Social hypnosis is their choice sis.

In those early dark days I'd pull the nuclear option and just get drunk son but I learned my lesson.

Some people are so elastic they show sins on their face. These ones should be celibate to ace.

Some people are so malleable they show sins on their face. These should be chaste in any case.

You proved your worth to her. When she was down you wouldn't help her in fact you spat on her.

Honey you were a cloud without rain. I postponed and waited but there comes a time to gain.

BE YOUR CHILD AGAIN

You need to be your child again--spontaneous and free--and that comes from repenting/forgiving.

No guilt or shame blocking creative circuits. Keep the slate clean: each dawn is a new beginning.

Honey you were such a cloud without rain. I got so sick of the empty promises/nonproductivity ok.

I don't care anymore what happened out there I'm a homey for life and you're not gettin' in here.

Religious leaders who do nothing to change your life due to false agendas & traditions of men: aye!

FOOLS & TRAMPS

They do not encourage your relationship with God just to go to all their activities "religiously".

Life is a pie but they don't encourage your inner journey adventure but the outer one: social culture.

Life is a pie but you can't spend your time expanding talents you must worship as they want it.

Maybe the men could work but the church ladies attacked me mercilessly for my liberties.

The death of anointed leadership started in the sixties and it's come to roost today in misery.

Could you look silly, catty or immoral when it's really just mental illness? Yes, in most cases.

YOU MAL-ADAPTED TO DYSFUNCTION

You mal-adapted to a dysfunctional family system or culture and the outcome was bonkers.

People know what they know and don't know what they don't know, that's what it comes down to.

Repent and forgive to be a child again. That's totally spontaneous without messes/new friends.

It's possible to be very clever and educated but still mentally ill: being smart doesn't mean well.

Don't fret past actions. If anything you taught em about mental illness but now you're back son.

Mental illness includes anosognosia: the inability to see one's own patterns, no changes/eurekas.

The witnesses are dead, the youngsters don't know you instead so now it's just enjoy retirement.

FOOLS & TRAMPS

You've crossed the great divide, Creative Act is locked in and the formula's written, bonafide.

They can't minimize you now, you're over the hump. The work is spectacular/your cred is up.

The Formula's locked into place and it's simple to know from afar: you've overcome, you're a star.

In times of transition [after an era of nothing happening] there is highest synchronicity believe me.

Suddenly all the irons on the fire started popping, after literally decades of thankless working.

If someone's an empty suit or a bucket of s**t you'll know it now cuz you've grown up so.

How much of it is warranted guilt and how much is imputed to you from hereditary dirt?

IDENTITY IS RELATIONAL

Since identity is relational, you're sudden growth threw them outa comfort zone, pushed down.

One feels crippled by being eclipsed by another who refuses to recognize them for whatever.

Since identity is relational these systems show constant struggles to maintain a rigid status quo.

Your ordained clientele will now arise as you the visionary magically pulls em outa hell.

With anosognosia you can't see your patterns and do insane, absurd things in a blackout.

In America we operate by contract, do it on time or say we can't do it: we don't hang people up.

FOOLS & TRAMPS

Tho' the biggest slut in town she was mentally ill with anosognosia and a haunted home.

Collapsed morals and boundaries equals the biggest slut in town as the evil world crashes in.

If you're mentally ill butter learn defense against all the men in town who have gotten an earful.

Collapsed morals/boundaries [most important in psychology] = degradation = relapse =death.

Unless rigid moral boundaries as learned in the church she can't defend herself/lost the hedge.

WITHOUT RIGID MORALS

Without rigid morals AND holy identity she'll be degraded and do anything they say.

Don't do what men ask you to. It's degraded now and they over-presume. Be bold and say NO.

Don't do what men ask you to, be bold saying NO too. It's degraded now and they over-presume.

DISGUSTING. You are disgusting but can't see it. You look silly promoting this dirt and I fear it.

Most famous writers in history were rejected early cuz in psychology everything's compensatory.

Sinfulness is mental illness. As William James said symptoms leave when there is repentance.

Addiction is clouding your vision with just one thing while everything else is blocked out.

There's a female demon and I was it. I didn't know it at the time but wow, what an indiscrete twit.

FOOLS & TRAMPS

I don't want this crap in my life. Either get hep and real or leave my side, I just don't have time.

It's all explained thusly: you were weak so Satan took over mind and body, now forget it honey.

It happened to all your persecutors too, Satan had taken over/it occurs for whole cultures.

That's why we gotta stay strong. It's the only hedge of protection against evil influencers around.

Being social is NOT a requirement for salvation so when they bug you do go here and there, tell em.

When you cave people distance themselves, that's just how it is as you slide down or relapse.

FIRST THEY LOOK GOOD

First they look like God then they most definitely do not. It's all from something they did like a nut.

God says I was with you through all that and this is your reward for overcoming your Waterloo.

We're the land of opportunity [turn something outa nothing] but not with this Joe Biden.

Because he won't listen to anyone but himself he stays ignorant. He just thinks "well I'm it".

Thirty years you won't get back cuz a relative you respected put you down like heck.

Your creativity was derailed for thirty years by a slump created by an evil kin you respected then.

I had to get thru twenty years of gut pain from attachment trauma before having a ball.

FOOLS & TRAMPS

Maybe had a nervous breakdown, coulda been mentally ill, how do I know way back then.

The key to success is to get outa Dodge. Away from those memories of a past/mere mirage.

People are so cruel the kids are blunted right away. That's where callousness starts ok.

I had a mental illness. About fifty it lifted and that's how come I got here, high paid as gifted.

YOU'RE CALLED A "CONTROLLER"

Sometimes we're attracted to our opposite--we'd call this a "growth cycle" which is true when you think about it.

You're gonna get hurt. This guy was a con job from day one. Sorry to say it but I gotta hurt you to help you hon'.

When they gaslight/call you a controller when you just want a respectful relationship, you're just being honest.

After a life of impositions nothing is more satisfying then home ownership cuz no interruptions/I rule the ship.

If your spouse is 80 years old with cancer, you stay with him. You don't leave for greener pastures like a bum.

If your spouse has aneurisms you don't leave him you make the environment totally tranquil and peaceful.

MICROCHEATING

If he ever fakes being single he is micro-cheating and you'd better see it and believe it, we've all been thru it.

If you're just going to a store and he's chatting the girls up, watch out. This guy's into porn too, the chump.

FOOLS & TRAMPS

TELL HIM: I'm doing my part. I'm crazy about you, am in love with you so I just need to know: is it **SAFE** to love you?

I mean I see you chatting up the girls, triangulating, showing off to the peanut gallery--am I seeing things?

Because in an honest relationship micro-cheating is **CHEATING** and the other's not cool darling.

We live in a weird sinful world and so the virtual dating world has a protocol and new way of viewing it all.

We're in an exclusive relationship, right? And so micro-cheating is obviously not alright, am I right?

An exclusive relationship should not be hurtful. If his actions are hurtful to you, re-evaluate the relationship girl.

Is it safe to love you? Cuz I gotta say the **ONE** thing that'll kill any and all attraction is that kinda behavior dude.

When the thrill is over it's gone and I don't want that to happen so do you think we can work on this?

MICRO-CHEATING ISN'T SEX

Micro-cheating is to gain attention/stroke one's ego. It doesn't belong in a committed relationship Joe.

Micro-cheating is not sexual nor a sexual act. It's **FLIRTING** that comes right up against it Jack.

The micro-cheater says "well we're not really having sex so there's nothing wrong" but there surely is Tom.

If one is compelled to publicly test how desirable they are to others how can the other feel secure? It is horrors.

If they start this stuff up or any indication of it, I'm gone and you should be too. Learn these scientific rules.

FOOLS & TRAMPS

It's not just that he's thirsty for attention but that he is so unfulfilled from within--you can't fix that ma'am.

Household rule #1: No one stays here--just our own family who never comes. Now you're in heaven.

Micro-cheating is unnecessary and disrespectful. Once we're set on that we can work on the rest pal.

You need to talk to your partner about your expectations--what do you need to feel safe and secure?

MALIGNANT FEMALE NARCISSIST

The malignant female narcissist is a frightening, dangerous witch. She'll stop at nothing if she's envious.

Pathological envy is her major characteristic. She doesn't just want ALL you have she'll ruin you for it.

With too much dietary fat I was reliving the past. Thought loops of ego deflation and frustration, no blast.

The malignant female narcissist often gets an army against you which she's bribed thru sexual expertise.

She's filled with confusion from the souls of men who used her and that translates to pure viciousness more.

Break connections if they're unaware, needy, weak, insecure, controlling, manipulative or condescending,

Deconstruct the snapshot [moment in time] making the relationship look sublime tho' not worth a dime.

Stop hanging onto the one who is a problem and you'll find the love of your life: that is the PATTERN.

My barometer: I was blissfully happy alone but when he came I never felt safe, comfortable or secure.

FOOLS & TRAMPS

The undeniable truth about how neurotic was my friend: she hated it when he came but still let him in.

They have everything to gain by making you look bad and cuz they're covert narcissists they don't even own that.

PASSIVE AGGRESSIVE ACTIONS

Passive-aggressive actions. Retaliation is hidden and manipulative, most times thru friends/relatives.

When the passive-aggressive covert narcissist fights you back it's always behind the scenes and bad.

Everything they do is to protect their image/facade so they must set you up to look bad, that's the gestalt.

Narcissistic behavior is when your actions don't line up with your words, it's like two parallel universes.

Most people love you until you're competition--then you'll see who your buddies are. Durianrider

If you live for people's approval then you die by their rejection. Durianrider

GUT ACHES FROM UNSTABLE GUYS

If you have to live with the consternation of your solar plexus going off wouldn't you rather be alone?

If constantly struggling with gut-aches you have ample cause to feel unsafe-- your inner True Self said it, ok?

"I see this behavior and it hurts me, making me really question the agreement we've got"--see?

I thought we were a couple, monogamous. But I see indications you're autonomous, please explain this.

Dumpers sometimes come back but you don't want em anymore so they get a dose of own medication.

FOOLS & TRAMPS

Tho' I'm mad over you I just gotta say those behaviors will kill ALL attraction and that'd be a misfortune.

I'm into healthy debate not pedantry. But with most women it's hard to tease apart truth, it's just tyranny.

STOP THINKING PAST LOWLIFES

Stop thinking of lowlife obstructers best forgotten. That was your Ph.D. in the streets, it had to happen.

Don't blame them blame your immaturity and low life level that gravitated you to them, cuz it's equivalent.

It feels so good to delete and block the past that never was. I wanted one but now feel utter disgust.

Being retired is falling out of structure. No more expectations--take off suit and slip into pajamas.

Feminists complain or rape but are ok with pornography--they aren't moralists, they just wanna bitch.

Women are lunatics: screaming like banshees, self-congratulating, raving evil killers of babies.

AO Cortez wants us to think she's intelligent but it's just word salad filled with trendy buzzwords, just a nut.

I pray the public's not so dumb to fall for this but they're SO dumbed and it happened in Germany, sis.

Forbidden suspensions of violent black thugs: If you remove consequences, get ready for the flood.

Sin makes a person "heinous": everyone hates him. It's all subliminal, a dark muddy aura and demons.

I'll never forget how I felt when everyone hated me. A stranger in a strange land, I was terrified and lonely.

FOOLS & TRAMPS

The great Beethoven was hated by schoolchildren in town. They tormented him daily and it kept him down.

AMORAL YOUTH SO UNCOUTH

When the youth/children with no morals, restraints or parents rise up to murder us all, it was all predictable.

They're mad blacks are in prison more but unable to see it's their BEHAVIOR not horrible racism or disfavor.

Welfare and integration never cured inequality because groups aren't equal but that notion's unacceptable.

It's extortion: If we give em more stuff, they'll change. Fifty years of failure and there's even more rage.

The more we give em the more it increases the problem.

Rescuing, blaming others for their actions, removing consequences: ENDEMIC in the black community.

The biggest lie of our generation is the hoax of black victimization and if you see the videos it's all gone.

DEFEATED BRATS SITTING IN WHITE

The women sat there in white like defeated brats and demonstrated they do NOT love America, the rats.

The white-clad baby killers at SOTU resembled spoiled angels of Satan. Childish, commies, manly women.

If you vote democrat after SOTU you're deliberately voting for evil: your heart hates good and God.

May God have mercy on your soul if you stay with the dems for karma will be terrible staying with them.

SOTU fiasco sure showed how immature and childish women have become. Dress alikes, come on!

FOOLS & TRAMPS

Amazing accomplishments--how could they not want that? You'd have to an enemy of America to not.

It is better to remain silent and be called a fool then to open your mouth and remove all doubt.

They lie even when they're caught. They just don't care, so brainwashed by all the lies they bought.

REESTABLISH THE OLD PATHS

Old movies are a symbolic repository of the era, a time-capsule so rare, so fascinating if you care.

Men used to be protective and respectful--very--of women but thanks to you feminists that's all ruined.

I'm anxious by the lies/brainwash coming from Crazy Cortez cuz people love lies in their fallen state.

Masculine confidence is seen as patriarchy so it's squashed by female-dominated everything.

Take your children outa class when you hear "equity", "diversity", "inclusivity", "white privilege" or "racism".

Women are annoying and they know nothing.

Crazy Cortez is not just a tool for a globalist carbon tax scheme but she's a manipulative liar too.

Pre-success crisis. Discouragement hits near the end--a test of faith: do you still call God your friend?

Feminism has taken over the churches and it's a disgrace. It means heresy, falling away: NEW AGE.

How easily women fall into paganism. They can't hold to true doctrine, they're into anything ear-ticklin'

FOOLS & TRAMPS

I hear "Christian" women talking of reincarnation. They don't know how to divide and give ear to lies.

Pagan women disgrace: Russian's queen gave ear to Rasputin and the whole oligarchy was killed/erased.

NO DOCTRINE JUST VIRTUE SIGNALING

It's never about the dollar amount so much as the leftist programs they wanna slip in: ouch.

With the left it's always a raw power grab masquerading as racial justice. They're the nicest/you're a racist.

Brain De Blasio releases thousands of convicts from prison then brags how few prisoners they have: hmm.

Evil ALWAYS wears white to be seen as holy cuz they're the opposite--but black is ministerial, get it?

Who wears black? Maestros, men in tuxedos, ministers. Who wears white? Unholy feminist monsters.

Anyone who would joyfully kill their kid is a demon from hell and that's what feminism surely is as well.

The End: Biden to destroy lovely suburbs by placing far-left bureaucrats to zone huge apartment buildings.

To save precious time, pick two opinion leaders and leave the rest. You're wasting time with the repetitious.

THE NEW CRAPPY WORLD

Like crabs in a barrel women hold each other down. Just when you're up they go to battle--Lord, come!

Ok, it's gonna be their world/we're on our way out. But we still gotta fight for what's right/elders have clout.

FOOLS & TRAMPS

Trump who's always ten steps ahead of the rest is preparing for civil unrest in the wake of mass arrests.

Crimes of deep state are so deep/wide they must put em thru military tribunals so they can't deny it/hide!

The democrats all scream "impeach" because it's all about covering up their dirty and dastardly deeds.

Whether republican or democrat, open borders people are full of crap. President Donald Trump

Rich liberals and wealthy donors are the ones for open borders. They're the worst hypocrites/murderers.

Open borders are dangerous and immoral. We aren't "all one" as traitors say, we're surrounded by devils.

Communism is the ruling ideology, socialism is the practical application of it. Keep that in mind.

5G is a murder weapon. It breeds viruses, it reduces oxygen in the blood, you can't breathe, on and on.

We don't have that kinda crap around here in a country neighborhood. We can't get cells--it's that good.

What is an American? Someone who loves freedom.

Our Herculean genius president is more magnetic, majestic, brilliant, shrewd cuz God's behind the dude.

THE NEW CRAPPY WOMEN

We've got to wake up to what women are all about now. Our civilization's at stake, it's a terrible blow.

If she's mad at you and has "anxiety" she has a right to kill your child to get back at you, unbelievably.

FOOLS & TRAMPS

They're "against patriarchy" but that's the easy/harder way cuz you'll never be broken--to be protected.

The women are manly and disdain femininity. If you shave your legs you're their enemy, whore of patriarchy.

Men if you can find a lady grab her quickly--never let her go cuz she's rare as rubies/you'll have tranquility.

The feminist wife will argue constantly, bring up non-issues, impose worldly views and bore you too.

Women get angry--often violently--if you disagree with their introjected narrative from lowminded trendies.

If I didn't show sufficient sympathy for her pet project or something else in her bonnet she'd rebuff it.

I have many sides all so distinct it's like multiple personalities which I use artistically or manipulatingly.

Women are emotional, men are logical so when women gulp narratives they become most irrational.

RUNAWAY FEMALES IN POWER

When you build your dreams on a frozen snapshot you must use your mind to deconstruct it: make it a dot.

Women aren't worried about "stepping on toes" as much as they are getting disapproval ya know.

With women it's all virtue signaling for which they'll do the craziest things to be seen as holy by earthlings.

Meant to be meek and humble women become monsters causing so much incredible trouble.

Kamela Harris is the best example of runaway females tormenting males in congress--beyond the pale!

FOOLS & TRAMPS

We must now divide from their ranks. We are totally disgusted, they stink! Reject, give God thanks.

Is there no evil they won't put up with? Democrats are devils: Baby murder-- that's the ultimate.

Most importantly beloved, stay away from people. Be the top 5% and have NOTHING to do with evil.

Do not eat with whoremongers or anyone involved with illicit sex. Have no association for sex sins are the worst.

FEMALE TYRANNY IS SO COMMON TODAY

As anyone under female tyranny can confess: It's a most miserable place cuz women are out of grace.

Men are unswerving doctrinally speaking. They can hold to the line while women can't = catastrophe.

Women are best when humble (leading by serving) but when they rise up it's only trouble/sad endings.

Women are emotional and when that's in power you have sudden decisions devastating the future.

Men are measured, poised, even. That's true power and it's succeeded in all history and seasons.

When women are arrogant in their false wisdom (feminist narrative) they become the worst harridans.

Women will make up their own rules. They're much like immature children, childish radicals and fools.

We come to a point where the ugly past comes "up" through ego-alien materia and we lose it in America.

There comes a point where you block everyone you knew cuz in human systems behavior's compelled on cue.

FOOLS & TRAMPS

God said He'd always provide one good friend. That's good cuz the path is lonely/always on the mend.

When harridans get in power, watch out! For there is none more cruel against foes, and they're nuts.

IT'S CRUEL WHEN EMOTION RULES

There is nothing more cruel than when emotion rules. We spend our lives recovering from mother fools.

"We could even say that if it's not for the common good, it's not actually good". Pope pushin' communism

Trump who's always ten steps ahead of the rest is preparing for civil unrest in the wake of mass arrests.

Races are not all "one"! They're all different cuz that's how God made em--it's a good thing, not bad hon'

We're not like them and they're not like us--get it? We're all different as God made us, not "racists".

I wanna be with my own kind and there's nothing wrong with that. ALL people seek similitude, got it?

It's how they treat the least of us--DOGS! We Americans are kind to animals and other cultures are NOT!

Wherever there is mass immigration I instantly think of the SCREWED dogs and cats in that area, man.

In general people from poor countries don't give a dam about dogs--and you wanna let them in? Dear God!

WOMEN, BE REASONABLE FOR A CHANGE

For a change, be a woman they can reason with. You act so arrogant cuz to you liberalism is self-evident.

FOOLS & TRAMPS

What a relief to withdraw from addiction to youtube videos cuz no matter how valuable it's me ya' know.

You're brilliant but talk too slow/too many pauses. Maybe for the dense that's ok but I gotta get on with it.

Freelee didn't win the debate cuz she flaunted her abortion--that put's her at the bottom, third-rate.

Feminists like Freelee are brazen in abortion insensitivity and that's gonna come back at em baby.

It's none of my business why you did it--you did it, that's all.

Stop remorsing over when you were controlled by the devil. It's over now--through Jesus it's invisible.

The left really believes it is ok to hate certain groups, that hate is totally justified, and it's bigoted NOT to.

This isn't the twilight zone it's America run by the demonic left, a festering cancer. Alex Jones

Gotta have a vaca from all this. It's endless--senseless--studying all these messes by the dems: asses.

Nothing addictive will ever bring you the thrill of just your own mind, creativity, work and special destiny.

I knew I loved God at 5, knew I was an inventor at 12, a salsa trumpeter from 13, a psych theoretician 28.

FORGET THE PAST, LOOK FORWARD TO A BLAST

Stop remorsing over when you were controlled by the devil--due to weakness you were especially vulnerable.

It's not enough to write a 100 books, they can't find you. Gotta turn on the engine with keywords too.

FOOLS & TRAMPS

Stop the outer (videos) and open to the inner (utter greatness you know)--now you're all aglow.

Meant to be meek and humble women become MONSTERS causing so much incredible trouble.

The most important realization for growth is that no one cares. No one gives a dam--you are that rare.

The more unique, revolutionary and novel the less traffic--at first. Then it takes off suddenly of course.

SEEK STABLE MEN

It's not an exciting man I want it's a stable one. Then I can create my own excitement and fun.

If I have to spend my energy figuring him out, forget it. It's stability, that's a good guy for me.

I don't trust easily cuz I fear Betrayal Trauma again, as other woman should if they think back to when.

Nobody's as interesting as your own mind, dig deep.

No one's as interesting as your own mind so stop these silly addictions as if you need them--the blind.

Stop all poli-videos cuz it's just transitory reality. It's ephemeral--seek instead eternal, as Einstein did.

SUDDEN SUCCESS!

Don't worry in the twinkling of an eye you'll be in success mode and never think about those jokers again.

Discouragement hits like a ton of bricks. That's when you must turn to God who knows all the tricks.

Self-publishing leveled the field and anyone can do it. But you must also market it then discouragement hits.

FOOLS & TRAMPS

Stop your frantic outreach and go to the Only One who can teach: God your Dad/Co-Creator: beseech!

Stop reaching out to those who don't care/can't help the rare. That's you, a discoverer with just a prayer.

Loved Joyce Meyers 20 years ago, avoided her (heresy accusations) but now she's lifted my desolation.

Many strange and unique predicaments happen to people--odd attachments or associations with evil.

Faith: a powerful force that changes things. It does things like cause us to enter the rest of God, our King.

DUNNING-KRUGER AND AOC CORTEZ

Dunning-Kruger Effect: The people who know the least are the most self-confident, e.g. AOC Cortez.

Lack of critical thinking in superficial arguments that are unrealistic but it sounds good and gov's behind it.

What matters is: she's a really good person, and *you're NOT*.

In that era we were supposed to give the kids self-esteem regardless, and we created this: AOC Cortez.

Motto of "customer's always right" combined with "our children are precious" creates entitlement culture.

YOUTH LACK CRITICAL THINKING

The youth push back against any criticism cuz they don't wanna use critical thinking to test em.

Not legal definition "US citizens" but "persons of the U.S.". Meaning: just show up to take my stuff.

AOC is not only dumb and ignorant but totally self-assured. The Millennials: "self-esteem"was their cure.

FOOLS & TRAMPS

Millennials never ask deep questions. The argument is: it sounds good, people support it so it's ok.

In entitlement culture, everyone gets the trophy, creating AOCs--called "great" though they are nasty.

YOUNG SOCIALISTS PISSED

Young socialists don't question socialist Venezuela cuz there's no critical thinking so to hell with ya.

In these crazy latter days it's an act of bravery to defend biology. Male and female for example, oh my.

The noble lie and climate alarmist catechism: we're dead in 12 years vs. utopia and guaranteed income.

As socialism enters under the flag of climate salvationism it's a spectacular sized government invasion.

AOC: We're gonna be dead in 12 years America vs guaranteed income of her envisioned utopia.

AOC Cortez: so much self-confidence while being an arrogant dumbass.

Sympathy for ISIS and MS-13 is at an all-time high with the left. From party of Lincoln to party of Marx.

Democrats are no longer the party of the working man but the party of free stuff, and socialism will be rough.

Why does AOC get press? Republicans are weaponizing her nonsense to make democrats look a mess.

Abortion insensitivity is brazenly disgusting typical of feminists.

Arrest Mafiosi Pelosi for treason--put her in GITMO with the Bushes, Obamas and the Clintons!

GOD WILL TAKE CARE OF IT—DON'T WORRY!

FOOLS & TRAMPS

Beauty for ashes, oil of joy for mourning, garment of praise instead of heavy burdened and failing spirit.

Instead of your former shame you shall have a two-fold recompense (double for your trouble payback).

In your land you shall receive double what you forfeited and everlasting joy shall be yours--THIS YEAR!

How to have faith: He's a God of Justice, which means He makes everything right in every case.

I didn't say which culture is cruel. Even the cruelest culture has enemies they castigate as "so cruel".

"He will give everything to you which is Mine but only as you mature and grow up in God" so work on self.

My big male dogs are terrified of my tiny female cat. Because she's OLD she knows, with perfect control.

Demons, toxins, wrong diet--there's various reasons for insanity, juvenile delinquency, tendency to riot.

In the church the only fun is eating so many are fat automatically.

You saw me at my worst but don't you understand it was DEMONS from association with the cursed.

If you don't see every moment as divine (a perfect plan or design) then you'll be wasting your time.

I eat what I want when I want--in the morning.

FORGIVE TO BE FREE OF THEM!

Forgive: Not because your enemies deserve forgiveness but because you deserve peace. J. Meyer

God destroys our enemies little by little and for the Christian every day gets brighter & brighter kiddo.

FOOLS & TRAMPS

Forgive darkness, God opens you to heaven's brightness. Do the impossible then achieve God's likeness.

America's a bad place, business is evil, redistributive policies work, socialism need be tried. AOC Cortez

When family comes before right and wrong it's evil: such nepotism seems impossible to break thru.

Hate, anger and resentment focuses you too much, you can't see God. Forgive to have joy--open up!

You go a long time but eventually the axe will fall. Though it was slow in coming you robbed us all.

FOR SPIRITUAL SOLACE—CHURCHES?

We need leaders who are not afraid of not being popular--to be bold and true forever.

Religious leaders aren't necessarily anointed. More often than not modern ones are off point.

Are you following religious leaders who can only give you rhetoric or the traditions of men?

For spiritual solace don't seek churches. They've all fallen as women have taken over, the witches.

Men are to rule the family and the church. But cowering before feminists they leave us in the lurch.

Modern church is a mixture of the liberal feminist narrative, new age, wicca/occult and social hall religion.

The modern church seeks unity--an evil concept--not division between good and bad or the toxic.

Since women are 80% of the church the sermon better be feminist or the lights go off: how unfortunate.

FOOLS & TRAMPS

The churches have fallen into false doctrine and it's all to please the feminine as men are no longer men.

If you want truth. God and doctrine don't go to a church. For they have fallen to Satan and under a curse.

AOC IS RACIST TO WHITE MEN

Alexandria Ocasio-Cortez is racist towards white men. There's no doubt about this, it's blatant friends.

If God wants me to have it I'll have it and if He doesn't I won't so I'll leave it there and cast my care.

Christian men believe in God's justice but the wicked hate it, squelch it and refuse to address it.

Good men crave omnipotent justice that no one escapes because they're rewarded/not on the take.

Sinners with a lot to worry about hate justice. They believe anything means nothing for instance.

The postmodernist leftist ideology is nonsense but because there's no critical thinking it's unchallenged.

The Green New Deal democrats are socialists. They are ANTI-Israel, Catholic, Jewish, firearm & infant.

Can't distinguish between made-up nonsense and scholarship: introject the trendy/never question it.

SEASONS OF LIFE

It's a journey manifested in different stages of life. You have seasons, some dormant/silent or strife.

There are seasons of planting, harvesting and don't forget: digging up foul ground (feels like tragedy).

FOOLS & TRAMPS

Paul said his **ONE** aspiration was to forget what lies behind. What a revelation cuz that problem is mine.

Look forward to heaven and forget all about the leaven--the resistances making you stronger than demons.

I know what I am and I know what I'm not and I've given it **ALL** to God. Joyce Meyer

Until success I shall listen to Joyce Meyer on success: how to wait without getting messed up.

God said He'd do It and I trust Him so I am happily expectant.

It's just too horrible everything I know so I must control my reality and cut out everything dark below.

Never have people been more offended. They're so touchy even breathing they won't talk to me.

Forgive to prevent Satan from having control over you.   2 Corinthians 1:10

God if I'm mad at anyone show me who it is. For I'll never be a success if I can't forgive my own sis.

In the end times many will be offended and they will stumble and fall: We can't afford anger anymore.

LOVING PEOPLE MEANS MERCY

To be good at getting along with people we must show mercy: That's harder than anything, you see.

Forgive real quick. i'm asking you to get a Master's Degree in forgiveness so life finally becomes bliss.

After he raped me 200 times by age ten, I forgave him and even took care of him until the end. Joyce Meyer

Forgiveness is the greatest blow to the kingdom of darkness.

FOOLS & TRAMPS

Do your responsibility--what you CAN do, then cast your care. Dave Meyer

Having done all the crisis demands, now just stand. Ephesians 6: 13

Jesus paid so we could enjoy our life--until it's overflowing with goodness--so let's get on with forgiveness.

What we focus on, we magnify. So for goodness sake, watch your mind, think of God then be happy.

Do not let yourself be overcome with evil but overcome (master) evil with good. Romans 12: 21

Don't cast the responsibility on God but then keep the care! Give yourself a break and become rare.

Do what I should not, don't do what I should: Feel like cleaning house then lie down on the couch.

That's why we don't go by feelings, as women do. What we feel is Satan going against logic/emotions rule.

UNRESOLVED ANGER: BLOW UPS

With unresolved anger we either blow up on outside, implode on the inside or scapegoat those on our side.

If God can't give me what I want then I have no business wanting it. Stop self-salvation/let God do it.

She had so much unresolved anger from the past locked up she mis-fired on the undeserving without stop.

No one can take success from me if God wants me to have it. Keywords and SEO or not, forget it.

Storms make trees grow deeper roots so don't fear what you went through to build great attributes.

You sound like a backstabbing neurotic not a Christian man. Bet you'll block me cuz you can't stand correction.

FOOLS & TRAMPS

I need no other entertainment other than my own mind. It's just amazing what comes through of Thine.

I've been hurt by women too so I understand why you hate it but if you catch me in the same web, shove it.

It was scary when my sister read Malcolm X in the sixties. The sick sixties began all these tragedies.

Talkiin' of shaved pussies saying he's a Christian--we're to remain unspotted in this world man.

IS THIS ONE?

You can smell his divisiveness. It's not raw truth he's saying its unkindness and haughty mercilessness.

And we're sick of this.

I got tired of being mad all the time cuz I chose wrong friends I refused to understand (bad men/women).

When God shakes things up everything false falls away and only the true stands: *these* are your friends.

God, even if I'm lonely please get every person outa my life who is not good for me. Shake it up Daddy.

People will only hold you down. They're a severe encumbrance, nothing is better with them around.

Chemical sensitivities keep me humble. I could never get too full of myself knowing how fast I tumble.

They were just there for a season, now let them go. They were sparring partners, resistance-foes.

There is nothing done by myself that more people makes better: my OWN company/remove fetter.

FOOLS & TRAMPS

God is a consuming fire. He'll shake it all up so just the true remains: elimination is the game.

You may feel lonely for a time cuz you have no friends--but God, the only One who mends/lends.

God give me godly people in life whom I can count on and trust! After what I've been thru, that's the gist.

Remove Obstruction = Giant Transformation. Wait on Lord, renew thy strength.

It may not be pleasant for awhile to be alone but honey later on--the most anointed time on the throne.

SOUL-SUCKERS

God knows and he'll take care of it. You're only confused if having to know what only God gets.

It's only because I'm mature/older that I sit pretty in a safe place with fence and locked gate--high border.

When younger I let people impose on me with porous borders. I'd let em in without vetting invaders.

As I matured I became formal. Appointments only, no casual drop ins, give me problems & out you go.

I felt so abused by my "guests". No one knows how to act anymore and will bog you down, the pests!

People = boring. Selfhood and solitude: enlightenment, happiness, soaring!

It took a lifetime to establish a safe home with locked gate or to even know I needed it or bad fate.

Above all, avoid virtue-signalers. These are the women trying to get attention in the fallen church (leaven).

In a minute they're convicted: Just by one word you said or grimace/raised eyebrow of the elected.

FOOLS & TRAMPS

There have been no penalties for hate hoaxes, only rewards.

The name of the game is: how to recover from a narcissist. These men pull you in then do you in.

You're pandering to the peanut gallery old man! To get their approval you sink to their level and are fallen.

SOCIALISM TAKES, CAPITALISM CREATES

The left wants to divide this country by race and thus it's always about the "white supremacist".

The woke FBI would rather have 1000 terror attacks than one would-be terrorist inconvenienced.

We've never met a "white supremacist"--that's just what the left spews out on a daily basis.

There is no white supremacy in this country but there's plenty of brown and black supremacy.

Socialism **TAKES** and capitalism **CREATES**. WHAT YOU'RE ESCAPING:

Like crabs in a barrel they keep each other down. Homeostasis: Being down brings pep-talks, being up brings insults. Thusly the sick system maintains itself.

<u>NOW YOUR TIME HAS COME</u>

LIFE STAGES: ARE YOU READY?

I pray the work of your hands will make an amazing new dent in culture or turn the ship around for sure.

Life stages of a person: starts unrefined then ends a true genius with a Creative Act of the rare kind.

Now the end occurs: completing old cycles and beginning new ones. Glide

FOOLS & TRAMPS

through the transition, it's fun.

Some people prefer a separate reality being alone with God and pets. They're not the herd but the eccentrics.

Clear the decks so God can give you what you want. You're blocked with distractions, that's my rant.

Secret to best work: *wait.* The superior man never acts unless cued--that's what makes him great.

People who judge you by your past don't belong in your present. So true--reject, or be soooo blue.

THE CREATIVE ACT IS BORN

You already had your Waterloo--humiliation, public opprobrium and loss--so now you're boss.

Suddenly irons on the fire started popping, after decades of thankless working/nothing happening.

Finally, hard work and assiduity wins out over image-magic, name dropping and social connectivity.

Finally I can strut my stuff after years hard-pressed to explain myself to the conformist crowd.

Home is most important as it insulates females from a callous world so their talents can unfurl.

Being "out there" was tortuous. Cruel, insensitive, insulting, using, invasive: I wanted marriage.

It's a matter of timing which is seasonal. If nothing's happening it ain't your time yet ya know.

WORTHLESS ACCOMPLISHMENTS

You wanna rush things with worthless accomplishments not work alone without brownie points.

FOOLS & TRAMPS

It's a hideous stigma to go way out and live in a shack to avoid their flack, can you overcome that?

Working alone you will be targeted. There's a conspiracy against privacy/they don't like it.

Your work and work until your craft becomes as natural as a bird singing, like it's in your DNA.

You perfected the technique so that now creative impulse flows thru unobstructed/best.

You've got your environment perfectly adapted as well, looks to me like you're ready to win girl.

Most importantly, you've made peace with and disencumbered yourself from the past, at last.

That's all I gotta say. Life's a bitch but you can skillfully navigate it with God & angels leading the way.

FIND YOUR TRUE REALITY

You follow gurus and mentors until you mature. Then you sift and decide for yourself: boss chair.

What are you getting out of this? Meaning, acceptance--or just filling time while destiny is missed?

Must just show up. You've studied, cried, overcome those who lied--now just shine as you reply.

Hold back (strength) until your time has come. Then it's power unleashed (never called dumb).

"Lord, turn it around!" Repent and return from the brink like Nineveh--then feel bliss like nirvana.

Pneumaticity is "leaving a space" which can now fill in. The best way to work is to just start chillin'.

FOOLS & TRAMPS

Fights are a case of wrong identity--you are misperceived and miscast as the enemy. Just be friendly, okay?

My favs are becoming boring to me. I'm sick of input: I want to create and from all outer chaos be free.

Search the net: what you're looking for isn't there. It's True Reality, but leave a space for prayer.

NEVER LET EM FRAME YOU

Friends and family may be on the other side. They refuse to face the truth so from you they hide.

Divorce all snobs--you must. For they feel superior but for you it's self-esteem or bust (only friends you trust).

By snobs your identity is framed and it's a lowdown thing being thusly chained. Reject, esteem reclaimed.

What to do when you see who he is: Don't get in a tiz for you knew it all along but stayed mind-fizzed.

It wasn't you being bad--you soaked it up like a sponge. That's how brainwashing makes us grunge.

He's the man giving me the life I love. That's reason enough to treat him well and be sweet as a dove.

For many life is in the pits. Don't let it continue--whatever you do, repent and shake the devil to bits.

Kids reflect mom's angry spirit but blame it on father--getting worse as feminism's more entrenched than ever.

Back down, don't push back. Now pray as God pours ashes on his head and his world turns black.

Women: don't push back but back down. For female power is silence then you wear the crown.

FOOLS & TRAMPS

SO YOU MADE A MISTAKE...

So you made a mistake. Just pray and watch God turn all-bad to all-good for those who have faith.

Compulsive behaviors are mental illnesses, even speaking loudly in public for attention is sickness.

Compulsive behaviors are from stress. Tho' a form of PTSD they should still be addressed (no finesse).

Like AOC Cortez cheering on twitter the LOSS of 25,000 high paying jobs—aren't dems getting bitter?

Ever notice how the compulsive also gossip? It's put-downs compensating shame in the closet.

ALL BEHAVIOR IS COMPENSATORY

All behavior is compensatory, psychologists say. Look deeper than symptoms--were they betrayed?

You've done nothing wrong but there's a war on your mind. That's why you often feel down, or unrefined.

Every woman is wise and foolish, clever and absurd, good and bad. It's a package deal: good vs. cad.

If there's nothing coming through the spout, don't write. The worst thing is to force things—it won't be right.

There were times in history where people became crude. Picking their nose, pissing in the street, lewd.

I have a mental picture of the concept in time, a phrase comes through and then I finish it with a rhyme.

Most everything is PTSD. Otherwise we'd just be normal, you see? It's a matter of obstruction: debris.

Problems like anorexia and bulimia are post-trauma stress disorders: fear is a

FOOLS & TRAMPS

robot out-of-order.

What is the trauma? Involvement with wrong people forming templates of self-despair even for the able.

You can't bring them up--they'll only bring you down. That's the reality of human systems vs. your crown.

LIFE'S PARADOX: MISSING THOSE YOU SHOULD BLOCK

Life's a paradox! Like missing wrong people you should block: they seem like doves but are hawks.

Most all problems come from people involvement. Left to your own these irritations would be absent.

Be there for them as the veil falls from their eyes. When they see the light you'll hear the gullible's cries.

I write what I feel, couched in what I think. It's my way to deal with emotions while we approach the brink.

Those with most to say are shunned, ignored and minimized to their dismay. Wait, you'll have your day.

Popularity is no proof of the truth--but you gotta speak it anyway so the youth line up at your booth.

Dad didn't say it was easy but that it could be done. Now get off your butt, hon--and get disciplined, son.

It's all just energy: dense vs. clear. The bio-drives (food/sex) become the most compulsive (no cheer).

For every sin there's a seed of compensation (punishment). God won't have to--it's inherent in the moment.

TAKE OUT THE TRASH

Take out the trash. Those people brought demons too and thus you feel bashed--now get back your dash.

FOOLS & TRAMPS

Tho' seen as heretics I'll stick with my brother and sister in Christ, Joel and Joyce and be so enticed.

Thru Joel and Joyce I'm learning how to wait for my lifelong work to be seen as great but if not it's OK.

My plans didn't work out, no worries I'll come back tomorrow cuz God still directs my steps and more.

Success is 90% attitude while we wait: Give up your control and lean on God THEN he opens the gate.

HYPERSYNCHRONICITY IN TRANSITION TIMES

What's shut up in your spirit is being released. Dreams, potential, promotion, healing and vindication.

Breakthroughs: the fullness of your destiny--crossing the great divide occurs in the twinkling of an eye.

Don't cry over past actors--their part in your story is over. God pruned them and now they're no more.

In times of transition the archetypes explode. Take advantage of this opportunity to reach your goal.

Wrote 82 books/gave em all to God. Not gonna make em an idol by focusing or fearing in a reality flawed.

Apart from Me you can do nothing. John 3

God said the number of my days He would fulfill. He has His plan for me so no matter what I'm happy still.

We're supposed to cast our care, not control it all. Release control and what a release of energy, WOW!

Sorry I missed your call. I'm making changes in my life and if I don't call you back, you're one that's all.

DON'T HANG ONTO OLD

FOOLS & TRAMPS

Don't hang on to the old. That doesn't mean they're a bad person but it's a new season--so be bold.

I don't need your doubt or to hear what I can't do--I'm gonna surround myself with a faith filled crew.

America is NOT a hateful country--it's the most welcoming place on earth. Reject those liars, a curse.

Decades in desert wilderness to sort out my bad fate. Overcame it all: a nice house/tall fence/locked gate.

High wall: each day is my own. All who enter are vetted/on probation forever-- mark of a leader I wager.

The books are done, no matter what they say. I don't have to defend em either, will retire all my days.

Now that I'm done writing about psychology I aspire to think only good things. I'm through with neurotics.

NO SUDDEN CHANGES

Can't make a sudden change, there are others to consider. I know you know this, it's being mature.

I've got to break through that iron wall between what I feel and what I express. Vincent Van Gogh

I think we'd be a creative lighthouse but I'm ultra-creative by myself. Whatever God wants will be best.

Love victim: I'd like to melt right into you but my trauma bond coach talked me out of it, saying to dial it all back.

It's not a waste of time to look out the window so do it and do it more. Never feel aimless or lazy, it's all inner.

See how productive not-working is. That's when you get the insights to continue, leisure's it!

FOOLS & TRAMPS

Take the day off to please God. All work (tunnel vision) and no play (envision) equals dullness (odd).

God has put you in a silent period where no matter what you're alone--a test before your star is shone.

BLESSED MONOTONY

The saints need monotony to create. Strict routines with rare deviation: that is the setting to be great.

Stop all outer entertainment and just think. Image success and a beautiful future, enough of the stink!

Enough of the political videos, you know it all anyway. Stop wasting time and just think, imagine and create.

Take a vacation from the poli-videos, they tire. Why? Cuz they're tracking your brilliant mind with inferior.

At first they enchant but soon it's just another boring tangent cuz the real prize is your own mind, get into it.

DIETARY CONFUSION: MEAT & LEAVES

How vacuous they must be to watch someone eat and talk of absolutely nothing from a head so empty.

Lowcarb or highcarb, high fiber or low fiber, fasting or no fasting, high sugar or low—will we ever know?

I've been a dieter all my life and tried all of em. It's a never ending search at the end of 112 books, welcome.

Raw or cooked, starches or fats, high-water fruits or caloric density for satiety: online debates are endless.

Fruitarians say fruit/rice most good, Gundry says avoid em for they poke holes in the gut/fecal leaks into the blood.

FOOLS & TRAMPS

Reversal Dieting: A carnivore with fruit vacations. I eat once a day meat & leaves with seasons of fruit and restin'

All you can do is learn all the diets then pick what works best or reverse/alternate between all of them I guess.

Sometimes high intelligence is a curse cuz in search of the truth you're forced to go to all this extra work.

Everyone has their ups and downs but when you're dwelling on trifles/being psycho-aggressive, it's DIET.

I'm so happy returning to fruitarian consciousness after having lost it thru the avocado murkiness.

Without dietary fat in the system I can dream again. It's a cornucopia, just as Ehret described in 1857.

A Californian addicted to avocado cuz it's cultural and really all they know may never experience the glow.

Fruit, fruit, rice, water, sleep: how simple. Avoid stimulants or you'll become a fat storer, reversing your plan.

LACTO-FRUITARIAN EARLY YEARS

You may live on lacto (raw milk and cheese) and forget the meat. That' was me in one meal a day, so neat.

I had gotten past the vegan mindset/agreed to eat meat yet the mind said NO until total depletion.

One can't go from salads & smoothies/fruit to carnivore diet without minor discomfort: low carb flue.

Meat and leaves once a day, I thought I could do it with eggs and cheese but no way. Protein pays.

What a relief after a lifetime of this crap: dieting, measuring, weighing but now I have the right map.

FOOLS & TRAMPS

Following diet experts took decades from life. These were valuable lessons, getting sick/filled with strife.

It's not any one diet but the reversals between em all. Enjoy life to the max, eat good food even fry it.

Food window 4 hours: Raw milkshake, baked potato w/butter/sour cream, fast 20 hours: totally keen.

The cows WANNA be milked. They need to be milked and there's a lot in there. They're like pets too, here.

Mother's milk is so nurturing, comforting, sustaining, strengthening but It's got carbs so abstain from it?

The bible recognizes meat eaters from those who abstain. I think it's just something in the DNA.

Vegetarianism: The Ghandi Diet was fruit, nuts and milk. That's where I'm at: nutbutters/cheese fills me up.

I'm through seeing diet scientifically but rather what I want today

DIET INSIGHTS THRU THE YEARS

When I said "I will eat what I want, when I want" my whole life opened up. In a blink, I felt on top.

People weren't into diets in the fifties and everyone looked like movie stars. They ate it all too I swear.

My neighbors have happy cows as milked pets. Delicious raw milk, cream, cheese and yogurt I get.

Immunity restored--just by eating what I want and avoiding what I abhor using fasting as the Magic Door.

I feel so much better now that I eat what I want when I want. Now I'm the doctor directing it.

FOOLS & TRAMPS

My acid reflux/low energy is gone by eating what they told me **NOT** to eat and refusing what they think.

The anorexic says: spud without butter. The good-lookin' spirited chick says: eat it then _**fast longer.**_

MY DIET JOURNEY

What to do with a skinny woman with wrinkled extremities: **FAST HER** and do it immediately.

Paul Bragg said Toxic Acid Crystals form in the extremities into the root. TAC is the basis for wrinkles too.

Like all tradition let your food-life be two-speed: regular daily routine vs. rare festival [if desired] meats.

Thusly you have the beauty from non-acid foods and escape vitamineral or protein depletion if it exists.

Toxic acid crystals manifest in itchy dry wrinkles. It's all dried mucus [acid] under the skin gone in a day or so.

No more sauerkraut and spuds. Potatoes and tomatoes are becoming impossible as nightshades: acid reflux.

Instead of reflexively taking an ant-acid, investigate why you have it: to culture food you're horribly allergic.

The simpler my diet to which I've adapted the more multi-variable I will be as a talented creative agent.

FOODS CAUSE OR BIND "UGLY" MUCUS

No more "natural cookies". Tho' made with coconut flour etc. they taste like dusty mildew/organisms creepy.

Make your own if you have a mind but I'd not get into all of that. Just eat one meal and lose your fat.

FOOLS & TRAMPS

If you want all those deep wrinkles go eat all that food. It causes em, Berg's tables prove it's ACID/mucus.

How could we possibly need food that deforms the human body that way? It's so ugly it cannot be healthy.

Forget the corn/spud unless you're starving. They're on the cusp and won't do that much damage darling.

Food Today: Three red grapefruits, one small avocado, three mangos, tab. almond butter, half coconut.

Get frozen fruits and fill several freezers. That's for smoothies then add coconut, superherbs and nutbutters.

The closest I get to a salad is cilantro in my guacamole and also tomato, green onion, garlic, lemon.

I just drink my guacamole green goddess breakfast as a pudding then I'm done: fruit, greens, fat.

I don't care if you drink or eat meat, have at it. I'm just talking about myself, it's personal not about all of ya.

Age doesn't have to deform you that way. There's no reason things should change, look at older Vietnamese.

THE UGLIFYING EFFECTS OF ACID

The effects of culture food are so uglifying no artist could stand it and just to escape it would do anything.

Like smearing oils and creams all over the dry wrinkled skin--it can all perfect but it's done from within.

When all the wrinkles left the body with a fruit diet everyone said I was gonna die from not eating meat.

That seemed to me a pathetic contradiction that the body could obviously heal, yet NOW it was ill?

FOOLS & TRAMPS

That's the problem: I'm not a narcissist but I am an artist and I couldn't stand it, the deforming effects of ACID.

If hungry an orange cleans the gut of all elements incurring the pain. It doesn't take much--try a fig or date.

NON-ERHETIST FRUITARIANS

Modern fruitarians didn't follow Ehret--he would never derail from fruit by stuffing with starches at night.

Don't listen to anyone. They'll say no nuts, no avocado, making you famished for everything ya' know.

A few nuts and avocado as your staff cuz you need the fat. Keep em ripening in refrigerator as your stash.

Let the cheese and dairy go for awhile. With just mucus-binding fruits lets see how you do: new style.

The fruitarian community became a dam Nazi tyranny and the forums were filled with arrogant meanies.

What food put me through: countless days/nights of acid reflux, burping, bloating but now I'm all new.

To escape them I became a vegetarian--including cheese. A French diet so to speak but still up a creek.

Roast a pig for your festival and pig-out on it. The rest of the time enjoy thy fruits/herbs to stay top notch.

Other than the rigid constraint to alkaline foods, no one's gonna tell me how to do my diet even a few.

It's called the Science of Beauty. It's not about makeup, a tan or hair. It's about proportions/tone/flair.

It's so boring: preparation and food time. It's so much easier just to fast and acclimate to the hunger pangs.

FOOLS & TRAMPS

STARCHIVORE PHASE [NOTES]

The Fruit and Fat worked and still works. But "what works best is Fruit and Starch [corn, potato, rice]: highest carb"?

Rice and corn may be least allergenic. Avocado allergy sets in easily: it's a latex allergy like bananas and kiwi.

With chemical sensitivity you must rotate your meals or become allergic. Avo every day = feel acidic.

I know of no one who's allergic to white rice. I'm making fried rice in my new pan and low fat is the plan.

Fruit, sugar, starch, water. You mean the superherbs don't matter, it's really ALL about carbs and sugar?

Many have reversed cancer with rice and fruit diet. I'm happily rid of acid-reflux, thorn in my side.

Pro-cyclists found the fruit diet was not enough for maximum energy/endurance but with rice it all changed.

They needed the complex carbs, the high glycemic index, the potent shot of carbohydrate, the quick sugar.

"Fatty Acids". Fat causes acid vs "Carbo-Hydrate": carbs and water [no acids]. I'll take the latter/feel placid.

Avocado causes acid-reflux not due to any latex allergy but to FATTY ACIDS in the blood constantly.

Gave my avocado stash to a neighbor and will now go fruit and rice without any more fatty acid horrors.

RAW 'TIL 4 MATRIX

How I went wrong: fat addiction and carb restriction. I'm back on the carbs and all oils/fats are gone.

FOOLS & TRAMPS

It's fruit, fruit, rice and no more allergic reactions or acid reflux. Being carbed up like this I really love.

How many fruitarians are addicted to avocados? With fat the cells melt together and the legs go too.

They use avocado and other fats to buffer against emotional realizations. They eat fat to deny these feelings.

Headaches, full feeling in gut, fatigue, lack of drive and ACID REFLUX from fatty acids. I repeat, fatty ACIDS.

We live in an age of lowcarb or keto everything. But Durianrider is right: fruit and rice is king.

Fruit, fruit, then rice. Last meal noon and here it's midnight and I'm not at all hungry enjoying the moon.

Ehret always said fats cause acid. With the fruit and rice the pain is gone: acid-reflux from the modern diet.

I've used avocado to blunt my emotions for decades. Eat rather than feel but without the fat I can SEE.

Go for the SUGAR not the FAT. And not just fruit either--you need the starches for a higher glycemic index.

Avocado held me back my whole life. Avocado: I felt nothing could be more natural but I was sluggish as hell.

Following Durianrider I had fruit then corn/rice and thought I'd die as it poked holes in my gut and sides.

LEAKY GUT: NO FRUIT OR GRAINS?

Then I looked up Gundry on leaky gut: no fruits, grains or nightshades. Who is right? I'm amazed.

ALKALINE. That's my major matrix and it means no fats/fatty acids. No avocado or sugar can't get into cells.

Leaky gut diet: broccoli, salmon, avocado, walnuts, blueberries. Fine, lets have this every day.

Because you love your pets that's who they'll target. Millions have been killed by kids vs. parents.

TRUST GOD SO CONFUSION GOES AWAY

It's amazing the problems that are solved just by the decision to trust God not yourself, I'm awed.

If you're confused you're not operating in faith cuz the moment you trust God confusion goes away.

When you trust God you don't have to figure things out anymore--no longer confused you can soar.

The less there is now the more there'll be later. Totally alone now = waves of mass attractions in future.

100 KAREN KELLOCK BOOKS

AFFINITY OR MISERY
AGELESS CORNUCOPIA
AMERICA AWAKE!
AMERICA'S DAFT ERA
ARTS OF PALEO FASTING
AUTOPHAGY ON CHEATERS
BACKSTABBING NEUROTICS
BETRAYAL TRAUMA
BOOMERS AND BROKENNESS
BOOT ON NECK
CHAMPION GUIDES
COMMIE NUTHOUSE
COMMIES
COMMUNIST SPIRIT
CONTAGION OF MADNESS
CONTAGIOUS MADNESS
CULTURE CLASH BASHED
DAFT LEFT
DAILY FASTARIAN
DAM RATS
DIVERSITY IS CRUELTY
E-RACE WHITE
EVIL FREAKS (Beyond Gross)
THE END OR A BEND?
FEMALE BULLIES AND FEMI-NAZIS
FEMALE CARNALITY
FEMALE DUMB DOWN
FEMALE POWER DRIVE
FEMINISM AND RUIN 1 & 2
FIX FOR MISFITS
FOOLS & TRAMPS
FREEDOM SPEAKING
FRENEMY ENABLER
FRENEMY LIAR
FRENEMY THIEF
FRENEMY TRAITOR
TRENEMY TYRANT
GENIUS IS HELD DOWN
GLOBALISLAM
GOD USES THE FLAWED
HAZE OF THE LATTER DAYS

KAREN KELLOCK PH.D.

Karen Kellock received her Ph.D. from University of California, Irvine and was a postdoctoral fellow at the Medical School, Dept. of Psychiatry [NIAAA and NIMH grants] to develop a theory of System Pathology: the Debris Theory of Disease, presented in 120 books and 22 textbooks for the general public. The theory has a general formula: All disease is obstruction, all recovery is elimination, all success is attraction. The three obstructions are people, habit and food. Remove your obstruction and snap to your goals, waiting in the wings.